WOULD YOU RATHER?

VALENTINE'S DAY
EDITION

RIDDLELAND

TABLE OF CONTENTS

INTRODUCTION

Welcome to the silliest, sweetest, most laugh-out-loud Valentine's Day adventure EVER! This isn't a mushy, lovey-dovey Valentine's book. Nope. This is the kind of book where:

- Cupid accidentally shoots himself in the foot (again),
- chocolate fountains turn into chocolate explosions,
- giant teddy bears don't just sit there: they walk, talk, and cause chaos,
- and your friends, pets, and favorite snacks show up in the wildest Valentine situations you can imagine.

Inside, you'll find 300 hilarious Would You Rather questions designed to make your Valentine's Day awesome, without a single cheesy poem involved.

This book is perfect for:

- playing at home
- sharing in the car
- classroom Valentine parties
- sleepovers
- or anytime you want to challenge your friends (or your parents!) to make ridiculous choices

Every question starts with "Would you rather..." and your mission is simple:

Choose ONE option. Even if both options are ridiculous. Even if neither option makes sense. Even if you burst out laughing halfway through.

You can play alone, with a friend, or with a whole group.

You can keep score, race to answer, or explain why you picked what you picked.

There's no wrong way to play; just lots of fun.

Get ready for:

- Candy chaos
- Weird magical mix-ups
- Animal Valentine adventures
- Glitter disasters
- And a grand finale that turns the whole book into an epic escape challenge!

If you're ready to giggle, think fast, and make the toughest silly choices of your life...

Turn the page and let the Valentine's fun begin!

HOW TO PLAY

Before you jump into all the Valentine's craziness: Cupid mix-ups, chocolate explosions, glitter storms. Here's how to play this game the right way (also known as the FUN way).

1. Pick a Question Reader
You can take turns reading aloud, or choose one person to be the "Question Commander."
Their job: read the questions with dramatic flair.

2. Choose ONE Option... No Escaping!
Every question starts with Would you rather...
Your mission is simple: Pick one of the two choices. Not both. Not neither. No sneaky loopholes. (Yes, we see you trying to find one.)

3. Laugh at Everyone's Answers
There are no right or wrong answers, but there are definitely hilarious ones. The best part of the game is hearing what wild choices your friends and family make.

4. Play With Anyone, Anywhere
Perfect for: family game nights, car rides, classrooms, sleepovers, Valentine's Day parties, kids who love silliness, and kids who PRETEND they don't love silliness. You can even play alone if you just want to sharpen your imagination.

Bonus Ways to Play

Level up the fun with these Valentine's-themed game modes:

Speed Cupid

You get 3 seconds to choose-no thinking allowed. Ready... set... PICK!

Explain-It Challenge

Everyone must explain why they chose their answer. Warning: You will not make it through this round without laughing.

No-Giggle Mode

Read the questions with a totally serious face. The first person to laugh loses. (Prepare to lose.)

Battle of the Choices

Two players argue why their choice is the better one. Everyone else votes on the winner.

Act It Out!

You must act out whichever option you choose. If your choice involves dancing, squeaking, pretending to be Cupid, or wobbling like a giant gummy bear... that's on you.

No matter how you play, there's just one real rule: Have fun and enjoy the Valentine chaos!

When you're ready, flip the page and jump into Chapter 1: Cupid's Crazy Warm-Up Round!

Chapter 1:
Cupid's
Crazy Warm-Up Round

Before you dive into the chocolate fountains, wild Valentine's parties, and magical mix-ups waiting in later chapters, Cupid wants to make sure you're officially warmed up.

But... since we're talking about Cupid, things might get a little unpredictable. His arrows might fly the wrong way. His wings might flap out of control. And his Valentine magic? Let's just say it's not exactly perfect.

So take a deep breath, grab your sense of humor, and get ready to survive Cupid's first round of silly chaos!

Here are your 30 warm-up questions: easy, funny, and just strange enough to prepare you for the wild chapters ahead...

Would you rather get hit with Cupid's giggle arrow  his dance-until-you-drop arrow?

♥ — ♥ — ♥ — ♥ — ♥ — ♥ — ♥

Would you rather catch a flying Valentine's card that smells like chocolate  one that smells like strawberries?

♥ — ♥ — ♥ — ♥ — ♥ — ♥ — ♥

Would you rather have heart-shaped freckles  sparkle-filled hair for an entire day?

♥ — ♥ — ♥ — ♥ — ♥ — ♥ — ♥

Would you rather wake up to 100 tiny Cupids singing outside your house,  one giant Cupid humming in your room?

— ♥ — ♥ — ♥ — ♥ — ♥ — ♥

Would you rather wear shoes that squeak, "I love candy!"  a hoodie that glows with flashing hearts?

Would you rather have a backpack that shoots out Valentine's cards  one that pops out pink and red heart confetti every time you unzip it?

Would you rather be followed everywhere by a floating pink balloon  a baby Cupid who keeps bragging about his aim?

Would you rather slip on a puddle of melted chocolate  fall into a mountain of pink marshmallows?

Would you rather eat a giant chocolate heart in one bite  a tiny chocolate heart that magically refills?

Would you rather have a Cupid sidekick who talks nonstop  one who only speaks in riddles?

Would you rather
have a heart-shaped shadow

or a shadow that blows
kissy faces at people as you walk by?

Would you rather
have a pencil that writes
in red sparkles

one that draws
chocolate swirls?

Would you rather get a mystery Valentine's card  a surprise candy heart in your pocket?

Would you rather wear heart-shaped sunglasses everywhere  glowing pink mittens that never turn off?

Would you rather sneeze tiny rose petals  tiny candy hearts?

Would you rather have Cupid's wings for a day  Cupid's bow (with silly arrows only)?

Would you rather have a locker that bursts with pink and red heart confetti  one that plays dramatic love songs every time you open it?

Would you rather have a talking teddy bear helper
who hands out tiny Valentine's

or a dancing flamingo sidekick who leaves
heart-shaped footprints everywhere?

Would you rather
only write with red pens
all week

only wear pink socks
all week?

Would you rather decorate the whole school with Valentine's balloons  bake 200 heart-shaped cookies?

Would you rather find a chocolate heart bigger than you  a tiny chocolate heart that keeps doubling in size?

Would you rather have a Valentine's card that keeps floating away  one that keeps sticking to your hand?

Would you rather carry a bouquet that keeps growing  a box of chocolates that keeps shrinking?

Would you rather accidentally turn your hair bright pink  your shoes bright red?

Would you rather
have a candy heart that grants one wish

or a Cupid arrow that
makes people laugh for 10 seconds?

Would you rather
have Cupid mix up his
arrows and give you
a squeaky voice,  make you speak
only in silly
Valentine's rhymes?

Would you rather
ride a giant teddy bear
to school  fly on a giant
Valentine's card?

♥ — ♥ — ♥ — ♥ — ♥ — ♥ — ♥

Would you rather
have a mailbox that teleports
Valentine's notes  one that reads
them out loud in
a goofy voice?

♥ — ♥ — ♥ — ♥ — ♥ — ♥ — ♥

Would you rather
get stuck inside a
heart-shaped bubble  in a giant cotton-candy
cloud that rains tiny
candy hearts?

♥ — ♥ — ♥ — ♥ — ♥ — ♥ — ♥

Would you rather
end the day covered in
sparkly Valentine's glitter  covered in melted
Valentine's chocolate
smudges?

Chapter 2:
Sweet Treat
Showdown

Welcome to the tastiest (and messiest)
part of the book!

In this chapter, the entire world turns into one giant
Valentine's dessert table. Chocolate fountains bubble,
cotton-candy clouds float above your head, and
someone definitely dropped too many sprinkles
somewhere...

Your mission: survive 30 sugar-powered questions
without getting stuck to the page.

Ready?

Deep breath.

Don't lick anything.

Here we go.

Would you rather swim in a pool of chocolate milk  bounce on a trampoline made of marshmallows?

Would you rather eat a heart-shaped cookie as big as your pillow  a Valentine's cupcake that's taller than your head?

Would you rather walk through a shower of pink gummy hearts  a blizzard of candy hearts?

Would you rather try a mystery Valentine's chocolate  a jellybean that changes flavors into different Valentine's treats with each bite?

Would you rather have pink Valentine's whipped cream hair  sneakers covered in heart-sprinkle frosting for a day?

Would you rather
eat chocolate-kiss ice cream that never melts

or cotton candy that stays sweet
and pink all day long?

Would you rather
own a mug that magically
refills with Valentine's hot
chocolate topped with heart-
shaped marshmallows,

a Valentine's candy bag
that always produces
one more candy?

Would you rather bake 500 mini Valentine's cupcakes  decorate one gigantic, school-sized heart-shaped cookie?

Would you rather have Valentine's frosting that changes flavors, like chocolate kiss, strawberry heart, and Cupid vanilla  sprinkles that change into every shade of pink and red?

Would you rather bite into a chocolate heart filled with caramel  one filled with gooey marshmallow?

Would you rather lick a giant heart-shaped lollipop  chew the world's biggest gummy bear?

Would you rather leave a trail of pink and red Valentine's sprinkles everywhere you walk  tiny chocolate-heart chips?

Would you rather
drink pink lemonade that sparkles

or cherry soda that makes
a tiny heart-shaped bubble with every sip?

Would you rather
eat a heart-shaped
pizza

a heart-shaped
pretzel the size of
a steering wheel?

Would you rather try a Valentine's heart cookie that can talk  a pink-frosted cupcake that can giggle?

♥ — ♥ — ♥ — ♥ — ♥ — ♥ — ♥

Would you rather wear a Valentine's candy-heart necklace that magically refills,  chocolate-dipped bracelets shaped like tiny hearts that never melt?

♥ — ♥ — ♥ — ♥ — ♥ — ♥ — ♥

Would you rather explore a maze made of giant heart-shaped jelly candies  massive chocolate kisses?

♥ — ♥ — ♥ — ♥ — ♥ — ♥ — ♥

Would you rather sip a pink Valentine's milkshake with secret toppings  eat a heart-shaped donut with surprise filling?

♥ — ♥ — ♥ — ♥ — ♥ — ♥ — ♥

Would you rather have red scented jelly lips  fluffy Valentine's marshmallow eyebrows?

Would you rather own a machine that creates
any Valentine's Day dessert you imagine - heart cookies,
pink cupcakes, chocolate kisses

or a machine that warms every
Valentine's treat to the perfect temperature?

Would you rather
have pink Valentine's
cotton-candy hair

a day OR hot-fudge
shoes that leave tiny
chocolate-heart footprints?

Would you rather drink Cupid's pink strawberry milk that makes you float,  Cupid's purple grape soda that gives you super speed?

Would you rather eat only red candy for a whole day  only pink candy for a whole day?

Would you rather have a heart-shaped waffle bigger than your backpack  a pink-frosted donut bigger than your pillow?

Would you rather try a sour candy that makes your voice squeak  a sweet candy that makes your voice extra deep?

Would you rather fill your backpack with giant gummy hearts  giant chocolate-heart bars?

Would you rather have a heart-shaped cookie that tells jokes  a brownie that sings love songs?

Would you rather drink a Valentine's smoothie with surprise flavors like strawberry-heart, cherry-kiss, or cotton-candy love  a hot chocolate with surprise toppings like heart-marshmallows, pink whipped cream, or chocolate-kiss crumbles?

Would you rather eat a Valentine's candy that changes flavor every bite, like a chocolate kiss, strawberry heart and cherry love  one that explodes with intense raspberry swirl flavor only once?

Would you rather end the day with pink Valentine's frosting in your hair  smudges from too many Valentine's chocolates on your cheeks?

Chapter 3:
Valentine's Day
at School

Valentine's Day at school is unlike any other day. The hallways look like a giant heart-shaped confetti cannon attacked them. Everyone keeps trading candy even though the teacher definitely said, "No candy until after class!" And the classroom pet hamster? Even it is wearing a sparkly red bow for some reason. Nothing makes sense today... but it's all hilarious.

This chapter drops you straight into the wild, sticky, glitter-filled chaos of a school celebrating Valentine's Day. Hold onto your backpack; things are about to get weird.

Would you rather have your teacher walk in dressed as Cupid  have your principal walk in dressed as a giant heart?

Would you rather open your desk and find it stuffed with candy hearts,  find a surprise Valentine's gift in there?

Would you rather walk into class and find the entire room filled with heart-shaped balloons,  find every desk wrapped like a giant pink-and-red Valentine's present?

Would you rather get a Valentine's card that shouts your name,  one that won't stop glowing bright pink?

Would you rather have your homework magically turn into a Valentine's poem  into a box of chocolate truffles?

Would you rather get a giant teddy bear from a secret classmate  a giant cookie shaped like your face?

Would you rather have your backpack refill with candy every hour  with colorful Valentine's cards every hour?

Would you rather have your classroom pet deliver the Valentine's  have the school mascot do it?

Would you rather have the cafeteria serve heart-shaped pizza  heart-shaped waffles for lunch?

Would you rather slip on spilled Valentine's hot chocolate in the hallway  trip over a trail of candy-heart wrappers?

Would you rather find a mystery
Valentine's slipped into your locker

or discover someone had pinned a thoughtful poem
about you to the outside of your locker?

Would you rather
have your pencil write
in red sparkles

pink holographic ink?

Would you rather have your lunchbox smell like chocolate  smell like sweet strawberries?

Would you rather wear heart-shaped sunglasses all day in classes  wear a giant Valentine's bow on your head?

Would you rather have your entire class do Valentine's karaoke  Valentine's-themed charades?

Would you rather have your desk lift a little higher each minute as pink hearts puff out underneath,  your chair spin once an hour when a Cupid arrow zips by?

Would you rather leave a trail of pink Valentine's glitter wherever you walk,  a trail of floating mini hearts?

Would you rather
sit in a chair that sings Valentine's songs

or one that blows
tiny heart bubbles when you move?

Would you rather
have every locker
decorated with
glowing pink lights

with giant
paper hearts?

Would you rather get a Valentine's card with a super silly cartoon of you,  a Valentine's poem that roasts your personality (nicely)?

♥ — ♥ — ♥ — ♥ — ♥ — ♥ — ♥

Would you rather have your notebooks smell like candy  your pencils smell like roses?

♥ — ♥ — ♥ — ♥ — ♥ — ♥ — ♥

Would you rather be surprised with a candy exchange  a surprise goofy-Valentine's gift swap?

♥ — ♥ — ♥ — ♥ — ♥ — ♥ — ♥

Would you rather watch the teachers dress as giant cupcakes  as giant love hearts?

♥ — ♥ — ♥ — ♥ — ♥ — ♥ — ♥

Would you rather have the art teacher accidentally spill buckets of pink glitter  buckets of love heart confetti?

Would you rather carry a backpack
that plays soft Valentine's music

or a backpack that shoots out pink sparkles
when you unzip it?

Would you rather
have your classroom
decorated with
giant teddy bears

giant paper hearts
that wave at people?

Would you rather have recess in a field full of giant heart-shaped balloons  giant Cupid-themed tunnels full of pink lights and floating hearts?

♥ — ♥ — ♥ — ♥ — ♥ — ♥ — ♥

Would you rather get caught in a hallway Valentine's parade  be dragged into a spontaneous classroom Valentine's dance party?

♥ — ♥ — ♥ — ♥ — ♥ — ♥ — ♥

Would you rather have the whole school smell like chocolate for a day  smell like roses for a day?

♥ — ♥ — ♥ — ♥ — ♥ — ♥ — ♥

Would you rather end the school day covered completely in pink glitter  covered completely in cute Valentine's stickers?

Chapter 4:
Cupid's Magical
Mix-Ups

If there's one thing everyone knows about Cupid, it's this: He means well...but his magic almost NEVER goes the way he planned.

He tries to cast a simple "spread kindness" spell...suddenly, the school hamster can talk.

He tries to deliver a Valentine's card...it grows wings and escapes through the window.

He tries to make someone's day sweeter...and now the cafeteria is raining candy corn for no reason.

Yep. Cupid's magic is powerful. Cupid's magic is sparkly. Cupid's magic is... a total mess.

This chapter drops you into the middle of Cupid's funniest and weirdest magical accidents.

Would you rather get hit with Cupid's arrow that makes you float uncontrollably,  one that makes you laugh so hard you can't stop snorting?

Would you rather wake up with glowing heart-shaped freckles  hair that sparkles every time you blink?

Would you rather have Cupid zap your backpack into a floating Valentine's suitcase with wings  your shoes into mini hoverboards that leave heart trails?

Would you rather sneeze out mini fireworks of Valentine's glitter  mini fireworks of pink heart-shaped smoke?

Would you rather have your voice turn into a Valentine's echo that repeats everything with "loooove" at the end,  a cartoon Cupid squeak that sounds like a squeaky heart toy all day?

Would you rather have your footsteps
leave floating pink hearts

or leave tiny sparkles
that follow you around?

Would you rather
accidentally cast Cupid
spells to make people fall in
love when you clap  when you sneeze?

Would you rather have Cupid's wings that flap wildly on their own,  his wand that sometimes works and sometimes does the opposite?

♥ — ♥ — ♥ — ♥ — ♥ — ♥ — ♥

Would you rather ride a giant flying Valentine's card  a giant floating love heart candy?

♥ — ♥ — ♥ — ♥ — ♥ — ♥ — ♥

Would you rather have a teddy bear that comes to life and follows you,  a Valentine's card that talks nonstop?

♥ — ♥ — ♥ — ♥ — ♥ — ♥ — ♥

Would you rather open a door to a magical candy world  a magical stuffed-animal world?

♥ — ♥ — ♥ — ♥ — ♥ — ♥ — ♥

Would you rather have Cupid accidentally clone you for a day  accidentally turn you invisible for a few hours?

Would you rather glow bright pink
every time you laugh

or float two inches off the ground
every time you smile?

Would you rather
get trapped inside a
ginormous heart-shaped
soap bubble

inside a drifting
cotton-candy cloud?

Would you rather have your Valentine's snacks magically refill forever, chocolate hearts, and strawberry gummies  your school supplies all be Valentine's shaped: a heart pencil-topper, pink-sparkly pen, heart-shaped post-it notes?

♥ — ♥ — ♥ — ♥ — ♥ — ♥ — ♥

Would you rather have a Valentine's unicorn whose sneezes spray sparkly heart-glitter everywhere,  a mini dragon that blows floating pink heart bubbles?

♥ — ♥ — ♥ — ♥ — ♥ — ♥ — ♥

Would you rather summon a rainstorm of rainbow sprinkles every time Cupid hiccups  a swirling snowstorm of tiny paper hearts whenever he sneezes?

♥ — ♥ — ♥ — ♥ — ♥ — ♥ — ♥

Would you rather have a shadow that can pull off silly Valentine's magic tricks (like turning pencils into roses)  a shadow that copies you five seconds late but giggles every time it catches up?

♥ — ♥ — ♥ — ♥ — ♥ — ♥ — ♥

Would you rather teleport by blowing a kiss into the air  teleport by doing a silly dance?

Would you rather
talk to animals for one Valentine's Day

or talk to objects
(like pencils and backpacks)?

Would you rather
cast Valentine's spells
only by singing a loud,
love-powered song

only by striking
a dramatic Cupid
pose that shoots pink
sparkles everywhere?

Would you rather have a wand that turns things pink  a wand that makes everything smell like chocolate?

Would you rather have your clothes magically change patterns  your hair magically change colors?

Would you rather have Cupid temporarily turn your bed into a giant marshmallow  your chair into a giant pink jelly heart that wobbles every time you sit?

Would you rather have wings that appear only when you're excited  a magic halo that lights up whenever you talk?

Would you rather send messages through floating sparkles  through tiny heart-shaped messenger birds?

Would you rather have Cupid accidentally make you glow in the dark  sparkle like a disco ball all day?

Would you rather find out your reflection can talk  find out your shadow can wander off on its own?

Would you rather create a spell that makes everyone silly  a spell that makes everyone extra kind?

Would you rather spend the day cleaning up Cupid's magical disasters  spend the day helping him create even more chaos?

Chapter 5:
Animals in Love
(and Total Chaos)

Animals don't celebrate Valentine's Day the normal way. They don't buy chocolates. They don't write poems. They definitely don't behave.

Instead... Penguins slide in delivering heart-shaped ice. Bunnies hop around, hiding sparkly cards under furniture. Pandas hug ANYTHING that looks remotely soft. And squirrels? Let's just say they've already stolen half the candy in town.

This chapter takes you into a world where animals throw Valentine's parties, deliver surprise gifts, and accidentally cause total chaos while trying to be adorable.

Ready to enter the cutest disaster zone ever?

Would you rather have a penguin slide up to you with a Valentine's card  a squirrel drop one on your head from a tree?

Would you rather get your Valentine's mail delivered by a hopping bunny a zooming puppy?

Would you rather dance with a flamingo wearing heart-shaped boots a panda wearing a glittery bow tie?

Would you rather have a cat write you a Valentine's poem a puppy paint you a Valentine's picture with its paws?

Would you rather ride a giant turtle carrying chocolates ride a giant bunny carrying flowers?

Would you rather have dolphins send floating heart bubbles  parrots sing you a cheesy Valentine's song?

Would you rather have a monkey steal your chocolates  a raccoon steal your Valentine's cards?

Would you rather get kissed by a baby goat with heart-shaped spots  hugged by a fluffy alpaca wearing a Valentine's scarf?

Would you rather have a goldfish blow heart-shaped bubbles  a frog hand you a candy heart?

Would you rather have a kangaroo deliver your gifts in its pouch  an owl drop them off at night?

Would you rather play fetch
with a giant teddy-bear dog

or fly on the back of
a giant lovebird?

Would you rather
have a penguin follow
you everywhere

a tiny piglet
that squeals
every time it's excited?

Would you rather have a chameleon that turns Valentine's colors  a hedgehog that puffs out tiny heart-shaped smoke clouds?

Would you rather watch a lion attempt to bake heart cookies  a hippo decorate cupcakes?

Would you rather get a Valentine's from a shy fox  from a llama who refuses to stop smiling?

Would you rather have bees spell your name in honey  ants build a giant candy heart just for you?

Would you rather get friendship advice from a wise old turtle  love advice from a dramatic talking parrot?

Would you rather run a three-legged race
with a kangaroo who, each time he hops,
leaves a trail of heart confetti

or a potato sack race with a polar bear cub
sporting a tiny Valentine's bow tie?

Would you rather receive
surprise Valentine's treats  from sneaky raccoons?
from sneaky squirrels

Would you rather have a bunny hand out your Valentine's cards  a cat arrange them perfectly on your bed?

♥ — ♥ — ♥ — ♥ — ♥ — ♥ — ♥

Would you rather give a Valentine's to a grumpy porcupine  to a bossy goose?

♥ — ♥ — ♥ — ♥ — ♥ — ♥ — ♥

Would you rather look after a unicorn-sized hamster covered in pink glitter  a dragon-sized goldfish that blows heart-shaped bubbles?

♥ — ♥ — ♥ — ♥ — ♥ — ♥ — ♥

Would you rather cuddle a giant sloth wearing a cozy Valentine's sweater  a giant puppy wearing heart-shaped sunglasses?

♥ — ♥ — ♥ — ♥ — ♥ — ♥ — ♥

Would you rather see mice perform a tiny Valentine's play  birds put on a Valentine's sky show?

Would you rather watch elephants spray
pink-tinted water

or dolphins perform
heart-shaped splash jumps?

Would you rather
have your Valentine's
delivered by a
galloping horse

by a bouncing
kangaroo?

Would you rather have a bear cub bring you a heart-shaped honeycomb  a fox bring you a bouquet of wildflowers?

Would you rather train a raccoon to wrap Valentine's gifts  train a parrot to write Valentine's jokes?

Would you rather walk into a room full of puppies wearing mini Valentine's bow ties  kittens wearing tiny Valentine's capes?

Would you rather spend your whole day inside a magical Valentine's zoo  inside a Valentine's pet amusement park?

Chapter 6:

Sweetheart Adventures Around the World

Grab your suitcase, your passport, and maybe a handful of emergency chocolate, because this chapter is sending you on a Valentine's Day world tour like no other.

Across the globe, people celebrate Valentine's Day in all kinds of unique ways...

But this version of Earth? Yeah, things are a little different.

In this world, Paris serves croissants the size of your face. Tokyo has vending machines that shoot out glowing heart candies. The Amazon rainforest hosts an annual monkey-led Valentine's parade. And somewhere in Italy, a chef is desperately trying to create the world's first pizza shaped like a perfect heart (he's on attempt number 243).

Buckle up; your global Valentine's adventure starts now.

Would you rather eat a giant heart-shaped croissant in Paris  a giant heart-shaped gelato in Rome?

Would you rather tour a magical Swiss chocolate factory  a Japanese candy lab with glowing desserts?

Would you rather ride a rose-covered gondola in Venice  a heart-decorated double-decker bus in London?

Would you rather have a Valentine's picnic under the Eiffel Tower  under floating cherry blossoms in Tokyo?

Would you rather watch a candy-confetti parade in Brazil  a giant-heart balloon parade in New York?

Would you rather
eat heart-shaped sushi in Japan

OR heart-shaped tacos in Mexico?

Would you rather
explore a Scottish
Valentine's castle

a Dubai candy palace
with glowing pink floors?

Would you rather walk through a glowing heart maze in Singapore  a floating lantern festival in China?

Would you rather ride a camel through a Valentine's desert fair  a husky sled through a snowy Valentine's village?

Would you rather take photos on a pink-sand beach in the Bahamas  in a heart-shaped flower garden in France?

Would you rather try magical Belgian hot chocolate  magical Taiwanese bubble tea that pops into hearts?

Would you rather have your name written in heart-shaped skywriting in Australia  in colorful flower petals in India?

Would you rather celebrate Valentine's Day
in a Greek ocean-view boat

or in a Costa Rican jungle treehouse?

Would you rather
see heart-shaped
fireworks in Dubai

glowing lanterns
float up into the sky
in Thailand?

Would you rather bring home a Valentine's teddy bear from Canada  a chocolate treasure box from Switzerland?

Would you rather go on a Valentine's treasure hunt in the Amazon rainforest  inside the Egyptian pyramids?

Would you rather try heart-shaped dim sum in Hong Kong  heart-shaped waffles in Belgium?

Would you rather watch penguins celebrate Valentine's Day in Antarctica  monkeys celebrate it in the rainforest?

Would you rather walk through a rainbow flower tunnel in the Netherlands  a lowing neon heart tunnel in South Korea?

Would you rather ride in a heart-decorated
hot air balloon in Turkey

or a Valentine's cable car
in San Francisco?

Would you rather
drink a mystery Valentine's
drink in Brazil

try a mystery
Valentine's dessert
in Japan?

Would you rather spend Valentine's Day on a snowy Swiss mountain  on a sunny Hawaiian beach?

Would you rather see a Valentine's water-fountain show in Las Vegas  a Valentine's light show in Singapore?

Would you rather explore a Moroccan candy market  a French pastry shop filled with pink desserts?

Would you rather get a Valentine's postcard from outer space  a Valentine's seashell from underwater Atlantis?

Would you rather travel in a magical Valentine's train across Europe,  in a magical submarine through coral reefs?

Would you rather explore a heart-shaped island  a heart-shaped forest full of glowing animals?

Would you rather try a dessert that changes flavors in Japan  one that changes colors in South Korea?

Would you rather dance at a Valentine's street festival in Spain  a snowy Valentine's festival in Norway?

Would you rather spend the day traveling the world with a magical Valentine's passport  exploring a giant Valentine's mega-theme park?

Chapter 7:
Valentine's Day
Party Gone Wild

Every Valentine's Day party starts normally... for about seven seconds. Then someone turns up the music way too loud. Someone else brings glitter even though everyone agreed "NO GLITTER THIS YEAR." A kid tries to juggle cupcakes. Someone spills pink punch in three different places. And suddenly the whole party turns into a chaotic, sugary, laughter-filled explosion of pure Valentine's energy.

This chapter drops you right into the middle of the wildest Valentine's party on Earth: complete with singing cupcakes, balloon disasters, and confetti that seems to appear out of nowhere.

Hold tight. This party has no brakes.

Would you rather walk into a party with 5,000 floating heart balloons  one gigantic balloon shaped like Cupid that keeps bumping into people?

Would you rather be in charge of handing out giant cookies bigger than plates,  cupcakes piled so high they wobble?

Would you rather fall into the chocolate fountain  send a full tray of cupcakes flying across the room?

Would you rather have heart-shaped bubbles float out every time you laugh  confetti explode out every time you say "hi"?

Would you rather join a surprise dance battle started by Cupid  a karaoke showdown where every song is about candy?

Would you rather have a DJ who plays slow romantic songs at MAX volume  fast dance songs that never stop?

Would you rather taste a mysterious pink dessert that wiggles  drink a sparkly punch that glows?

Would you rather get glitter stuck in your hair  frosting stuck between your fingers?

Would you rather play Valentine's charades, where every clue is super embarrassing  Valentine's trivia, where every question is weirdly hard?

Would you rather have a Valentine's goodie bag overflowing with candy  overflowing with mini toys?

Would you rather enter a room filled
with living giant teddy bears

or floating balloons that follow you around?

Would you rather
accidentally set off a
confetti cannon during
quiet time

activate a bubble
machine in the middle
of a speech?

Would you rather have a DJ dressed as a giant Valentine's cupcake  a giant Cupid?

Would you rather win a giant heart-shaped pinata  a mega-sized mystery chocolate box?

Would you rather get caught in a slow-motion bubble storm that pops into tiny hearts  a super-speed sprinkle tornado that blasts Valentine's colors everywhere?

Would you rather have snack bowls that magically refill  decorations that rearrange themselves every minute?

Would you rather drink punch that changes colors  punch that makes tiny bubble hearts fizz up?

Would you rather sit at a table
that slowly spins

or in a chair that hops every 10 seconds?

Would you rather
wear a giant Valentine's
hat shaped like a heart

a glowing pink cape that
swishes loudly?

Would you rather catch a flying cupcake  catch a flying Valentine's that zooms like a boomerang?

Would you rather start a chocolate fondue food fight  a sticker-tag battle where everyone tries to tag you?

Would you rather pop a balloon that explodes with candy hearts  one that explodes with rainbow glitter?

Would you rather decorate the world's largest Valentine's cookie  frost the tallest Valentine's cake ever made?

Would you rather lead the Valentine's conga line  lead a dramatic Valentine's slow-motion march?

Would you rather eat a cupcake
that sings a love song

or drink a punch
that giggles when you shake it?

Would you rather
wear glowing pink socks
that won't turn off

heart-shaped
sunglasses that
won't stop blinking?

Would you rather walk into the party and be showered with rose petals  be blasted with pink tissue paper streamers?

Would you rather play freeze dance with Cupid as the referee,  musical chairs where the chairs slide around on their own?

Would you rather end the party covered in edible glitter  covered in chocolate smudges?

Would you rather stay at the party for an extra hour of total chaos,  take home a mysterious Valentine's surprise box with unknown goodies?

Chapter 8:

Friendship, Kindness
& Heart Challenges

Valentine's Day can be wild: Chocolate fountains exploding, bubbles floating everywhere, glitter showing up in places no one can explain...

But underneath all that silliness, Valentine's Day is really about people: Your friends, classmates, teammates, and even that one kid who always borrows your pencil and never gives it back.

This chapter turns friendship and kindness into a game: fun choices, silly challenges, and "good deed dares" that make you think, laugh, and maybe even do something awesome for someone else.

No mushy stuff. Just pure, feel-good fun.

Ready? Time to test your friendship superpowers.

Would you rather make a funny handmade Valentine's for every friend  design a silly digital one for everyone?

Would you rather give out candy hearts with weird messages  stickers with goofy doodles you made?

Would you rather surprise a friend with a mystery Valentine's gift  be surprised by one?

Would you rather help a friend finish their Valentine's cards  rescue them from a decoration disaster?

Would you rather cheer up a friend by telling your sweetest, silliest Valentine's joke  by sharing your funniest fail story that always makes them smile?

Would you rather do
one huge Valentine's kindness challenge

or five mini kindness missions
that spread love all day long?

Would you rather
team up with a friend
to win a Valentine's
scavenger hunt

to complete
a wacky Valentine's
obstacle course?

Would you rather give someone a Valentine's note they REALLY need OR receive one you didn't expect?

Would you rather have a friend bake you a treat OR draw a Valentine's-themed comic starring you?

Would you rather trade Valentine's gifts with a friend OR create matching Valentine's crafts together?

Would you rather help someone carry a giant Valentine's gift box OR clean up a confetti explosion they caused?

Would you rather plan a surprise for a friend OR let a friend plan a surprise for you?

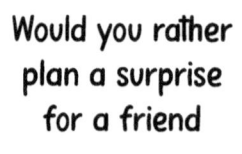

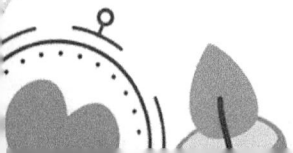

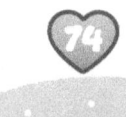

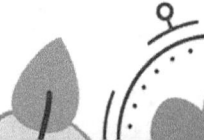

Would you rather write
a Valentine's message to future you

or to younger you?

Would you rather
spend the day doing silly
friendship challenges  building the world's
weirdest Valentine's
project together?

Would you rather get a sincere compliment from your best friend  give one that makes someone blush with happiness?

Would you rather help a shy friend hand out their Valentine's  help an excited friend calm down?

Would you rather have a friend share their favorite Valentine's snack with you  share your favorite snack with them?

Would you rather team up for a Cupid's escape-room challenge full of love notes and hidden hearts,  a friendship mystery puzzle that reveals a new act of kindness with each clue?

Would you rather thank someone who helped you this year  surprise someone who hasn't gotten much attention?

Would you rather
share a giant heart-shaped cookie with a friend

or split a huge box
of chocolates?

Would you rather
help a friend win a
Valentine's contest,

them help you win?

Would you rather make matching friendship bracelets  matching decorated cookies?

Would you rather team up to build the world's biggest Valentine's craft  bake the world's biggest Valentine's dessert?

Would you rather get a Valentine's filled with hilarious jokes  one packed with awesome compliments?

Would you rather compete in a challenge to do the most heart-warming acts of kindness,  a creativity challenge where you make the sweetest, most friendship-filled creation?

Would you rather be the "Valentine high-five giver"  the "Valentine's nickname inventor"?

Would you rather make people smile all day  make people laugh all day?

Would you rather be known for giving the best Valentine's  for making everyone feel included?

Would you rather have a friend remember a kind thing you did  a funny moment you shared?

Would you rather end Valentine's Day with an unexpected new friend  an unforgettable adventure with old ones?

Chapter 9:
Valentine's Day
Disasters

Some holidays are calm. Some holidays are peaceful.
Valentine's Day? Not even close.

This is the day when chocolate fountains erupt, balloon
arches collapse, decorations attack innocent students,
and tiny confetti pieces somehow end up in your socks.

It's not anyone's fault... Well... except Cupid's. And maybe
yours. And definitely the glitter. Welcome to the
hilarious disaster zone known as Valentine's Day.

Your mission: survive it.

Would you rather slip on a puddle of melted chocolate  slide across the floor on a pile of pink glitter?

Would you rather have a giant heart balloon explode above your head  have a balloon animal fall apart in your hands?

Would you rather watch your Valentine's card fly out the window  fall directly into the punch bowl?

Would you rather knock over the chocolate fountain  accidentally hit the "turbo mode" button?

Would you rather spill a bag of candy hearts in slow motion  spill sprinkles at lightning speed?

Would you rather have your goodie bag rip open in front of everyone, 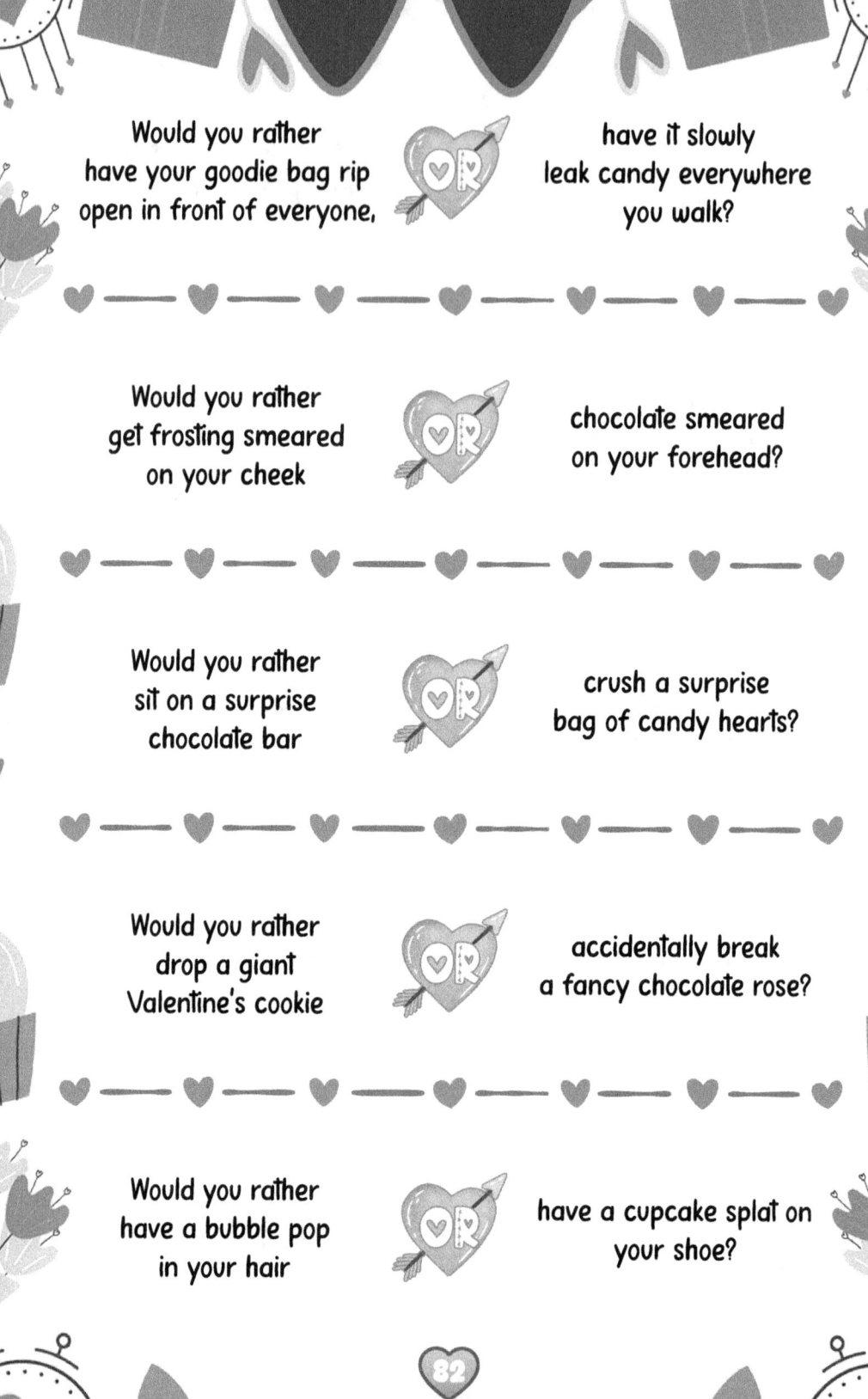 have it slowly leak candy everywhere you walk?

Would you rather get frosting smeared on your cheek OR chocolate smeared on your forehead?

Would you rather sit on a surprise chocolate bar OR crush a surprise bag of candy hearts?

Would you rather drop a giant Valentine's cookie OR accidentally break a fancy chocolate rose?

Would you rather have a bubble pop in your hair OR have a cupcake splat on your shoe?

Would you rather
get tangled in 20 feet of pink ribbon

or stuck inside a giant cardboard heart?

Would you rather
forget where you put your
Valentine's bag

accidentally grab
someone else's
identical one?

Would you rather trip while carrying a giant teddy bear  drop the teddy bear on someone by accident?

Would you rather blow up a pink Valentine's balloon that suddenly pops with a giant BOOM!  a heart balloon that squeals, wiggles, and zooms away as the air escapes?

Would you rather smudge all your handwriting  misspell every single name on your Valentine's cards?

Would you rather take down a giant Valentine's banner by mistake  have it fall on top of you?

Would you rather end the day covered head-to-toe in glitter  covered head-to-toe in chocolate frosting?

Would you rather sneeze
and send cards flying

or sneeze and make balloons float away?

Would you rather
drop your homemade
Valentine's in mud

smudge all
the writing
with sweaty hands?

Would you rather have your pet chew your Valentine's  your sibling "decorate" them with crayons?

Would you rather spill a huge bowl of bright pink Valentine's punch  knock over an entire tray of heart-shaped treats in front of everyone?

Would you rather accidentally knock down a balloon arch  take down a streamer curtain with your backpack?

Would you rather pop a giant balloon by accident  deflate one very loudly in the quietest moment?

Would you rather discover a chocolate stain spreading on your shirt  glitter stuck in your hair forever?

Would you rather
drop cupcakes upside down

or drop your carefully
made Valentine's craft?

♥ — ♥ — ♥ — ♥ — ♥ — ♥ — ♥

Would you rather
mix up who gets
which Valentine,

accidentally hand
someone two while
skipping another person?

Would you rather have a heart sticker stuck to your back all day,  walk around with a streamer trailing behind you?

Would you rather spill your Valentine's snack every time you stand OR spill your pink drink every time you laugh?

Would you rather get stuck in a storm of flying Valentine's cards OR a blizzard of pink tissue paper?

Would you rather get harmlessly hit by candy hearts OR harmlessly ambushed by a confetti popper?

Chapter 10:
The Great Valentine's
Escape Game

You've battled glitter storms. You've outrun balloon avalanches. You've survived magical disasters, party chaos, animal mayhem, and flying desserts. Now there's just ONE challenge left.

Legend says that deep inside the North Heartlands lies the Great Valentine's Maze: a shape-shifting labyrinth powered by Cupid's leftover magic. Every year, the maze wakes up for one day only... and traps whoever dares to enter. Tonight, it's awake. Tonight, it's hungry for chaos. And tonight... You stepped inside.

Walls slide. Floors bounce. Doors sing off-key. Cupcakes march in formation. Balloons whisper your name for no reason. And somewhere in the maze, a giant teddy bear is definitely plotting something.

To escape, you'll have to make choices: fast, funny, and very, very brave ones. Welcome to the final challenge. Good luck, Valentine's hero.

Would you rather enter the maze through a glowing heart-shaped gate  through a swirling pink vortex?

Would you rather carry a magical map that keeps telling jokes  a silent map that rearranges itself every minute?

Would you rather follow a trail of floating pink neon arrows  a trail of chocolate truffles that hop away when you get close?

Would you rather face a giant teddy bear guard who is too friendly  a Cupid guard who is way too dramatic?

Would you rather ride a moving heart-shaped platform that zooms around  climb a wiggly marshmallow staircase that jiggles under you?

Would you rather dodge sliding walls decorated
with giant glitter hearts

or a room with
pink bouncing floor tiles?

Would you rather
pick up a heart-red licorice
key that stretches

a glittery rock-candy key
that keeps cracking?

Would you rather get clues from a grumpy Cupid statue  from a singing Valentine's card that tries too hard to rhyme?

Would you rather run from a rolling pink boulder the size of a car,  dodge confetti rockets shooting from the walls?

Would you rather cross a floating heart bridge that tilts  a cupcake bridge that giggles when you step on it?

Would you rather push a giant chocolate block shaped like your face  pull a teddy-shaped lever that squeaks loudly?

Would you rather solve Valentine's riddles given by a genius owl wearing tiny heart glasses  from a super-hyper squirrel who talks so fast even Cupid can't keep up?

Would you rather be chased
by bouncing gift boxes

or by balloon animals
that keep squeaking your name?

Would you rather
take a shortcut through
a glitter tornado  through
a cotton-candy fog?

Would you rather face dancing gummy hearts that keep trying to hug your ankles,  marshmallow people who wobble around so much they bump into each other like giggly jelly towers?

Would you rather float across a room with Cupid's wings  zoom across on a giant cookie snowboard?

Would you rather open a door that blasts heart-shaped bubbles  one that rains down rose petals?

Would you rather carry a glowing heart crystal that hums  a magic chocolate bar that whispers clues?

Would you rather get stuck in a loop of singing doorknobs that sing only love songs,  a loop of dancing pink floor tiles that wiggle and shuffle under your feet?

Would you rather take advice from
a suspiciously wise guinea pig wearing a tie with pink hearts on

or a raccoon who insists he's "seen this maze before" and
he keeps holding his paws in a heart shape to show 'love'?

Would you rather
sneak past a room full of
snoring teddy bears

tiptoe through
a river of sticky
slime hearts?

Would you rather dodge arrows that make you laugh uncontrollably  ones that make you float up to the ceiling?

Would you rather climb a tower made of stacked Valentine's cards  a tower made of giant strawberry donuts with sprinkles raining down?

Would you rather sneak past guard lovebirds wearing tiny helmets  guard bunnies doing intense warm-ups?

Would you rather escape through a slow-opening, dramatic door covered in glowing hearts  drop through a trapdoor that launches you into a heart-shaped balloon pit?

Would you rather race a giant teddy bear to the finish,  race a flying Cupid?

Would you rather solve the final puzzle with a heart-shaped piece  an arrow-shaped piece that keeps spinning?

Would you rather have the maze congratulate you with fireworks that spell your name,  with heart-shaped pink and red confetti cannons that never seem to end?

Would you rather exit into a massive Valentine's celebration with music and treats,  a peaceful room filled with endless snacks and fluffy couches?

Would you rather stay in the magical Valentine's world for more adventures...  return home carrying the official title: "VALENTINE'S MAZE MASTER."

CONCLUSION

You Did It, Valentine's Hero! Wow. Look at you go! You didn't just read this book; you adventured through it. You dodged chocolate disasters, survived balloon chaos, befriended animals, cracked magical mysteries, won wild party challenges, traveled the world, and escaped the Great Valentine's Maze like a true legend.

That's not easy. But you made it look fun. This book was never just about choosing between silly options: it was about using your imagination, laughing with the people you care about, and discovering new things about yourself.

And the coolest part? Your answers created your own unique Valentine's story. No one else's version is exactly like yours. Maybe you changed your mind along the way. Maybe you argued your choices with friends. Maybe you cracked up so hard you couldn't even answer. That's perfect; that means you played the game exactly right.

The adventure doesn't end here. You can flip back to any chapter, play with someone new, make different choices, or turn the whole book into a challenge show. Every round becomes a brand-new Valentine's journey.

Thank you for bringing your creativity, humor, and heart to these pages.

You're officially a Would You Rather? Valentine's Day Champion, and the world could use more fun-makers like you.

Until our next adventure... keep laughing, keep imagining, and keep choosing the fun path.